FRANKLIN D.
ROOSEVELT

FRANKLIN D. ROOSEVELT

JEREMY ROBERTS

⌐LERNER PUBLICATIONS COMPANY / MINNEAPOLIS

For Ann Figundio

Lerner Publications Company
A division of Lerner Publishing Group
241 First Avenue North
Minneapolis, MN 55401 U.S.A.

Website address: www.lernerbooks.com

Library of Congress Cataloging-in-Publication Data

Roberts, Jeremy, 1956–
    Franklin D. Roosevelt / by Jeremy Roberts.
        p.   cm — (Presidential leaders)
    Includes bibliographical references and index.
    ISBN: 0-8225-0095-7 (lib. bdg. : alk. paper)
    1. Roosevelt, Franklin D. (Franklin Delano), 1882–1945—Juvenile literature.
2. Presidents—United States—Biography—Juvenile literature. [1. Roosevelt, Franklin D.
(Franklin Delano), 1882–1945. 2. Presidents.] I. Title. II. Series.
E807 .R615 2003
973.917'092—dc21   2001007208

Manufactured in the United States of America
1 2 3 4 5 6 – JR – 08 07 06 05 04 03

CONTENTS

———— ✧ ————

Roosevelt spends a quiet moment at his home in Hyde Park, New York.

INTRODUCTION

*"All that is within me cries to go back to my
home on the Hudson River."*
—Franklin D. Roosevelt, 1944

As a young boy in the 1890s, Franklin Delano Roosevelt often watched the Hudson River wind its way through the hills near his home in Hyde Park, New York. The view had a wonderful power for the boy. A glimpse of a sail might remind him of his seafaring ancestors. The whistle of a train from the rails at the shore could propel his thoughts into the endless possibilities of the future. The view remained important to him all his life. When he grew older, he arranged his bedroom so he could see the river first thing in the morning.

For Roosevelt, the Hudson River Valley was both inspiration and home—although fate would take him far. As a young man, he fought a disease that left him crippled for life. Later he led the United States through the Great Depression and World War II (1939–1945), two of its most difficult crises. Again and again, Franklin returned to

Hyde Park to restore not only his energy but also his vision of the country.

Franklin Delano Roosevelt had many qualities that made him a great president and a powerful leader. None were more important than his ability to remind Americans of the most important lessons he learned as a child, gazing at the river. As the river showed, a future built on a solid past can truly be unlimited.

CHAPTER ONE

A SWEET, DARLING BOY

"He liked to kick and feel free to move about."
—Sara Delano Roosevelt,
describing her son, Franklin, in a letter

The cold air held a promise of snow on the morning of January 30, 1882, as the doctor made his way to the front door of the large house in Hyde Park. Edward H. Parker entered and went immediately upstairs, his calm steps convincing the nervous family that he had everything under control. His pregnant patient, twenty-seven-year-old Sara Delano Roosevelt, had spent the night in labor. If things went well, her child would be born in a few hours.

But things didn't go well. Morning became afternoon, and afternoon faded into night. Still the baby remained in Sara's womb. Parker tried everything he knew—even yelling encouragement. Nothing helped. Dr. Parker gave up on the baby and concentrated on saving Mrs. Roosevelt. Even that seemed unlikely. The nurse whispered to herself that both child and mother would soon be buried. Then at 8:45 P.M., a large, ten-pound infant emerged—blue, starved of oxygen—but clinging to life. Dr. Parker blew air into the baby's mouth. The little boy breathed, then began to cry. His mother, too, revived.

The child's seemingly miraculous entrance into this world foreshadowed a lifetime of drama and challenge. The infant born that cold night before a snowstorm was Franklin Delano Roosevelt.

THE ROOSEVELTS

The boy's parents, Sara and James, took several weeks to name him, perhaps partly because their family histories presented many possibilities. James's ancestors had been in America since the mid-1600s and included an early alderman in New York City and a delegate to the New York Constitutional Convention. Franklin's mother, Sara, claimed she had descended from noble Romans and medieval knights. While most historians call those claims "tenuous," the Delano ancestors did include a *Mayflower* passenger as well as successful seafarers, merchants, and businessmen.

James was born on July 16, 1828, at Mount Hope on the north side of Poughkeepsie, New York. In 1853 he married Rebecca Brien Howland, who was distantly related to him on his great-grandfather's side. A son named James Roosevelt Roosevelt, called Rosy by friends and family, was born in 1854. After several years of failing health, Rebecca died of heart disease in 1876.

Tall and slim, Sara Delano's beauty attracted several suitors, but she spent most of her emotion and energy on her father. Blinded in one eye and then crippled by an accident, his health was poor for much of her adult life. She said later that she had been prepared to remain single before she fell in love with James Roosevelt, who lived only a few miles north of the Delanos' Hudson Valley home. At fifty-two, James was twice her age when they married in 1880, but the age difference was not considered an obstacle at the time. The couple traveled widely, rode horses often, and loved rowing on the Hudson.

DOTING PARENTS

The Roosevelts were well off, though they never possessed the huge fortunes of other Hudson Valley neighbors such as the Vanderbilts. Trained as a lawyer, James worked as

———————————— ✧ ————————————

Sara Delano and James Roosevelt, a few years before their marriage. The two met at a dinner party in 1880 and were married five months later.

general manager of the Cumberland and Pennsylvania Railroad and was a director of the Consolidated Coal Company of Maryland. He served as vestryman (a member of the governing board) and senior warden for his church and even as town supervisor, the head position in town government.

Franklin's arrival changed much for the family. Both parents doted on him. "He is such a fair, sweet, cunning little bright five-months-old darling boy," wrote a relative after visiting. "Mr. Roosevelt is very proud of him and Sallie [Sara] devoted and looks so very lovely with him." James took his son sledding practically from the time he could walk. They rowed together, skated, and raced iceboats on the frozen river in winter. He also taught Franklin how to hunt and sail. A photograph taken in 1888 at the Roosevelts' summer home in Campobello, off the coast of Maine, shows him at the wheel of his father's yacht. Franklin pursued quieter hobbies as well, collecting a wide range of objects. One of his favorite hobbies was his stamp collection, which he continued for the rest of his life.

James Roosevelt believed strongly in hard work and thrift. "There is not so much to luck as some people profess to believe," he claimed. "Indeed, most people fail because they do not deserve to succeed." At the same time, "Mr. James" recognized that there were not enough jobs for everyone who wanted to work. He also believed that all people, rich and poor—but especially the rich—had a duty to help others.

"The poorest man, the daily worker, the obscurest individual shares the gift and the blessings for doing good. It is not necessary that men should be rich to be helpful to

This 1888 photo shows six-year-old Franklin and a playmate piloting a yacht near Campobello.

others," he told his fellow parishioners at St. James Episcopal Church in Hyde Park. "Help the poor, the widow, the orphan; help the sick, the fallen man or woman, for the sake of our common humanity."

A SELF-CONFIDENT CHARMER

As a young man, Franklin charmed others easily. His self-assurance and good humor helped him put strangers quickly at ease.

In the winter of 1892, when he was about ten, Franklin went to visit the Pruyns, family friends in Albany, New York. Fourteen-year-old Huybertie "Bertie" Pruyn and her

*Franklin, pictured here with his parents at their estate in
Hyde Park, learned to appreciate outdoor sports at a young age.
He began riding ponies as soon as he was big enough.*

————————————— ✧ —————————————

friend Erastus "Ratty" Corning III were sure that Franklin
would be a spoiled prig. They hatched a plan to put him in
his place. "I can trip him up so he won't know what happened and then wash his face," suggested Erastus. He
packed a snowball for the ambush. "He's [Franklin's] probably a New York sissy."

They waited with their tobaggan until their guests
arrived. Young Franklin bolted over to them immediately.
"May I go coasting with you?" he asked enthusiastically.
Then he ran for the toboggan.

"Our guest was no sissy," said Bertie later. "He soon showed us he knew more about all kinds of coasting than we did, and he turned hand-springs down the [tobaggan] slide."

NOT A SAILOR'S LIFE

As Franklin grew, his love of the sea deepened. At about age thirteen, he began to think he would like to captain a ship. He wanted to join the navy. One day at breakfast, he suggested to his parents that he might attend the

———————— ✧ ————————

In this 1895 portrait, Franklin looks more like a young country gentleman than a sailor.

U.S. Naval Academy in Annapolis, Maryland. His father's expression turned grave. James soon led his son away to a private room for a man-to-man talk.

The life of a sea captain was not for Franklin, James said sternly. It wasn't just that James wanted Franklin to follow in his father's footsteps, attending Harvard University and then law school before going into business. A navy career would require Franklin to be away from his parents too much, James said. They loved Franklin too much to let him go. Franklin did not argue. While he would love the sea his whole life, Franklin loved his parents more and submitted to their wishes.

CHAPTER TWO

ELEANOR AND TEDDY

"I like 'fear nothing, be faithful unto death'
but I must say I wonder how many of the poor
mortals could act up to that."

—Franklin D. Roosevelt in a letter to Eleanor
Roosevelt before their marriage, discussing a line
from a poem she had sent

Sixteen-year-old Franklin grabbed the newspaper so eagerly
he nearly ripped it apart. He didn't have to hunt for the
article he wanted—the front page was filled with the events
taking place in Cuba.

It was 1898, and the United States was at war with
Spain. According to the newspaper, a cavalry (horse-mount-
ed) unit known as the Rough Riders had just beaten the
Spanish troops at San Juan Hill in Cuba. At their head was
former New York City police commissioner, state assembly-
man, and assistant secretary of the navy, Teddy Roosevelt.
Teddy was a member of the Oyster Bay, Long Island, New

Theodore Roosevelt
——— ✧ ———

York, branch of the Roosevelt family and one of Franklin's cousins. Teddy's war exploits were making him a national hero.

Franklin was a student at Groton School, a private school about thirty-five miles northwest of Boston, Massachusetts. Franklin had begun attending when he was fourteen, joining his graduating class two years after most of its other students. Until then, he had studied at home, mastering a variety of languages and other subjects.

At Groton, Franklin had to work to fit in with the other boys. Still relatively small at five feet three inches tall and weighing a bit more than one hundred pounds, Franklin was surpassed by his classmates in most athletic events. But the fact that he was related to Teddy Roosevelt enhanced Franklin's reputation at school. He emulated his famous cousin in many ways. Franklin adopted some of Teddy's expressions, such as "bully," which meant roughly what "cool" means. When Franklin needed glasses, he got a pair of gold-rimmed pince-nez—eyeglasses that clip to the bridge of the nose—just like his cousin's. He wore the same style for the rest of his life.

Groton students were required to play football. By his last year at the school, Franklin (front row, second from left) was among the better players.

———————————— ✧ ————————————

Franklin thrived at Groton, doing well in his studies, especially in Latin. By the time he graduated, he stood nearly six feet one inch tall. Like most Groton boys, Roosevelt went to college at Harvard University in Cambridge, Massachusetts. Franklin spent more time there socializing than studying, and he received more Cs than Bs. He did work on the school newspaper, the *Harvard Crimson,* and was elected editor, an important honor. James Roosevelt died in 1900, but Franklin continued his education as his father had wished.

Teddy, meanwhile, was elected governor of New York in 1898 and vice president of the United States in 1900. When President William McKinley was assassinated in 1901, Teddy became president. Franklin continued to admire Teddy and visited him as often as he could. Soon he had another reason to visit the Oyster Bay side of the family—Teddy's niece Eleanor, who also happened to be Franklin's distant cousin. It took only a few meetings for him to fall in love.

ELEANOR

Born in 1884, Eleanor described herself as a "shy, solemn child even at the age of two." Her father, Elliott Roosevelt, was Teddy's brother. Her mother's family was also wealthy, descended from Irish immigrants who had made a fortune in real estate. Eleanor's mother, Anna, died in 1892. Her father, plagued by alcoholism, passed away in 1894. Eleanor and her brothers were raised mostly by their maternal grandmother, Mary Hall. A "stern and pious woman," Mrs. Hall was extremely strict with her grandchildren. "We were brought up on the principle that 'no' was easier to say than 'yes'," recalled Eleanor. Educated in England, Eleanor grew into a tall, shapely young woman with a plain face and a generally shy manner. She and Franklin met several times when they were young—including once at Hyde Park when Eleanor was two and Franklin carried her around on his back. The two weren't close, however, until they met at parties as young adults.

In the fall of 1903, Franklin asked Eleanor to marry him. "Though I was only nineteen, it seemed an entirely natural thing," Eleanor said later. She was deeply in love,

*Eleanor in 1898, the year before
she went to study in England*

———————— ✧ ————————

and her letters to him often included love poetry. Sara
approved of Eleanor but thought her son was too young to
marry. She tried to dissuade the couple but was only able
to get an agreement from Franklin to postpone the wed-
ding for a year.

MARRIAGE
On March 17, 1905, Eleanor walked slowly down the
stairs of a home on East 76th Street in New York City.

The house, owned by Mrs. E. Livingston Ludlow, adjoined the home of Eleanor's cousin Susie Parish and Susie's husband, where Eleanor had been living. Eleanor wore a long, white satin gown. Her Brussels lace veil fluttered with each step. She leaned heavily on the arm of the man who was to give her away—her Uncle Ted, the president of the United States.

A select group of family waited in the drawing room of the Manhattan home. The bride took little notice of them as she headed toward her groom and the man who was to marry them, the Reverend Endicott Peabody, Franklin's rector at Groton. Outside, crowds waited for a glimpse of the president.

"Who giveth this woman to be married to this man?" asked Peabody. "I do!" boomed Teddy, and the rest of the ceremony and celebration rushed by in a swirl. Teddy was the center of attention, but the newlyweds didn't mind.

Before and after Franklin's marriage, he, like Teddy, moved in a circle of rich and influential people, insulated from most hardships. He took for granted opportunities that many Americans could only dream of. Like many others, he could be prejudiced about social groups and people who were not as well off as he was.

On the other hand, Franklin believed strongly in what he called the true democratic spirit. He defined this in an essay he wrote on his family's history while he was at Harvard: "[The Roosevelts] have never felt that because they were born in a good position they could put their hands in their pockets and succeed. They have felt, rather, that being born in a good position, there was no excuse for them if they do not do their duty by the community."

CHILDREN AND TRAGEDY

When the newlyweds returned from an extended European honeymoon (postponed until the summer of 1905 because of Franklin's law school classes at Columbia University), Eleanor and Franklin moved into a house in Manhattan. Sara had chosen and decorated the house and hired three servants. Franklin's mother could be very overbearing, but for quite a while Eleanor remained unsure of herself and may even have welcomed her mother-in-law's direction.

Soon after the newlyweds got back, they discovered that Eleanor was pregnant. Anna Eleanor Roosevelt was born on

─────────────── ✧ ───────────────

Franklin and Eleanor vacationed at Campobello with Sara in May 1905.

*Franklin and Eleanor hold their two oldest children,
James (left) and Anna (right).*

✧

May 3, 1906. A second child, James, was born on
December 23, 1907. On March 18, 1909, Franklin Jr. came
into the world—"the biggest and most beautiful of all the
babies," thought his mother. But Franklin Jr. and the other
children came down with the flu that fall. The infant died
November 8. His mother and father brought him to the
small churchyard at St. James Episcopal Church, where
Franklin's father had been buried. They watched numbly as
the small coffin was slipped gently into the cold, hard earth.

"How cruel it seemed," thought Eleanor, "to leave him out there alone in the cold." Both parents were deeply affected by Franklin Jr.'s death. They would, however, have other children: Elliott, born September 23, 1910; a second Franklin Jr. on August 17, 1914; and John on March 13, 1916.

POLITICS

In the meantime, Franklin had decided to run for the New York state senate. Like his father, but unlike Teddy and most of his neighbors, Franklin was a Democrat. The senate district included Columbia and Putnam Counties as well as Dutchess County, where Hyde Park was located. At the time, no single newspaper or radio station covered all of the large, rural area. Television had yet to be invented. To meet potential voters, Roosevelt came up with a novel idea: He campaigned by car.

Franklin was unstoppable. He went almost everywhere in the district and talked to anybody who would listen. With help and tips from the Democratic candidate for Congress, Richard E. Connell, Roosevelt won 15,708 to 14,568. Even to this day, he remains one of the few Democrats ever elected in the area.

As state senator, Roosevelt made a name for himself by battling corrupt politicians, especially Tammany Hall, a group of leaders from New York City who dominated the Democratic Party. While the group could count on many votes from working class people, bribes were more important to them than political ideals. And they did little to solve the city's problems. By opposing Tammany Hall, Roosevelt tried to follow Teddy's example.

EVOLVING SOLUTIONS

While Roosevelt was in the state senate in Albany, he pondered the role of government and the individual in society. In a 1912 speech he gave in Troy, New York, he tried to sort out the relationship between the two. Free individuals, Franklin believed, have a duty to the community. Government can help them fulfill that duty. Working people and business owners must cooperate. And, like his cousin Teddy, he said that trusts or monopolies were "evil" if, but only if, they benefited "a few" against the "interests of the many." Franklin's evolving political ideas included a strong religious sense of good and evil. His ideas were also influenced by farmers' struggles. He knew a lot about these struggles because many of his constituents were farmers, and his family farmed the Hyde Park property.

Many people were affected by the larger issues that concerned Roosevelt. Conflict between different social classes simmered throughout the world. Changes in the economy were causing severe hardships for many American workers and farmers. In Europe similar conflicts resulted in the rise of socialism, communism, and nationalism. Roosevelt's ideas did not make him popular with other politicians or guarantee support from the voters. When he decided to run for reelection in 1912, Franklin found himself facing a three-way race. Franklin looked forward to a vigorous campaign.

Then he came down with typhoid fever, a highly contagious and serious disease. He couldn't campaign. He couldn't even get out of bed.

LOUIS HOWE

In the autumn of 1912, a middle-aged man walked along a

deserted stretch of the Massachusetts coast at Horseneck Beach. Barely five feet tall, skinny, with a large head and scarred face, Louis Howe chain-smoked cheap cigarettes as he made his way up the beach. He squinted against the sun, heading toward a general store where he could pick up messages.

Howe had spent the last few months looking for work to support himself, his wife, and their two children. He was a former newspaperman, but his knack for politics had led to a promising job with a political group some months before. The job had fallen through, however, when the group's backer withdrew funding. Since then, Howe had mostly wandered the beaches near the small cottage he owned in southeastern Massachusetts, waiting for answers to job inquiries.

He had sent one of his letters to Franklin Roosevelt. When Louis Howe walked across the creaking floorboards of the general store on that particular day, a telegram from Franklin's wife was waiting for him at the register. She wanted to know if Louis could come to New York to help run Franklin's campaign for reelection to the state senate. That letter changed Louis Howe's life forever—and Franklin Roosevelt's.

TWO GENIUSES

Franklin Roosevelt was charming, handsome, and articulate. He had a knack for communicating ideas simply and effectively. These skills were critical for political success. Howe's skills were different. He knew how a politician should maneuver among different factions (groups) and how a politician could use issues to win votes. In short, he knew how to win political campaigns. Together, Franklin Roosevelt and Louis Howe were a formidable team.

While Roosevelt recovered from typhoid, Howe masterminded his 1912 reelection campaign. His innovations included sending letters on key issues to nearly all voters. This type of mass mailing is still an effective and important strategy. Roosevelt won by an even wider margin of victory than he had won the first time he ran. There was only one problem. By the time the election was over, he didn't want to go back to Albany, New York's state capital.

NAVY SECRETARY

Before the election, Roosevelt had supported Woodrow Wilson's bid for the Democratic nomination for president. Wilson was one of the most prominent reformers in the Democratic Party. At the time Franklin was running for state senator, Wilson was campaigning for the presidency. When Wilson won, he offered Franklin several jobs in the new administration, including assistant secretary of the treasury. But there was only one job—assistant secretary of the navy—that Franklin wanted. He soon got it.

"All my life I have loved ships and been a student of the navy," he told his new boss, Secretary of the Navy Josephus Daniels. Before going into politics, Franklin had practiced admiralty law, or the law of the sea, so he had a wide understanding of naval matters. There was also another reason he was attracted to the post—Teddy had held it from 1897 to 1898. Franklin, thirty years old, couldn't help but think he was following in his cousin's footsteps.

Teddy had been an active and at times insubordinate assistant. So was Franklin. In 1914, just two years after

Assistant Secretary Roosevelt (right, holding his hat), *accompanied by Eleanor* (rear), *reviews the U.S. fleet in New York's harbor in 1918.*

Wilson was elected, World War I started in Europe. Unlike the president and most of the country, Franklin wanted the United States to join the war. He often clashed with his boss and many others in the government over how large and how aggressive the U.S. Navy should be. He even suggested that the United States wage war with Mexico when that country's president was overthrown.

AN AFFAIR

While in Washington, Franklin fell in love with Eleanor's secretary, Lucy Mercer. Historians have theorized that he needed the "warmly intimate companionship" Mercer supplied. In contrast to Eleanor, Mercer seemed more carefree and less rigid. She was more attractive than Eleanor as well.

It's not clear when the affair began, but Eleanor found out about it in 1918. When she was helping Franklin unpack after a trip, Eleanor came across Lucy's love letters to him. Eleanor and Franklin argued bitterly over his affair with Lucy. Eleanor offered Franklin a divorce, but that would have ended his political career. In addition, his mother threatened to cut him off without a cent. Franklin agreed to end his relationship with Lucy, but the affair devastated Eleanor and changed their marriage forever. However, Eleanor stood by her husband in the coming years. He supported her, too, and encouraged her independence.

VICE PRESIDENT?

On the night of May 29, 1919, Franklin rose from the large banquet table in a hotel in Chicago, Illinois. Democrats from all over the country were gathered for a meeting of the Democratic National Committee. Roosevelt made his way to the podium with a smile, then launched into a speech he had written only a few hours before.

With the presidential election still a year away, he spoke about wider issues facing his party. Since the end of the last century, he said, there had been a great battle between progressives and reactionaries—or liberals and conservatives. The battle had now been decided. The progressives had won in the Democratic Party. The reactionaries had won in the Republican Party. "So we are approaching the campaign of 1920. . . with the broad principles settled in advance; conservatism, special privilege, partisanship, destruction on the one hand—liberalism, commonsense idealism, constructiveness, progress on the other," he declared.

The speech exaggerated tendencies in both parties, but it won Roosevelt national attention. With Howe's help, Franklin managed to make peace with Tammany Hall yet remain independent. The next year, Franklin backed the Tammany candidate for president, New York governor Al Smith. And when Smith lost the presidential nomination to Governor James M. Cox of Ohio, Roosevelt became the Democratic vice presidential nominee.

A campaign poster from 1920 for the Cox-Roosevelt ticket

Franklin asked Eleanor to accompany him on a campaign trip in 1920. Their marriage had recently been rocked by Franklin's affair with Lucy Mercer.

Cox was crushed by Republican Warren G. Harding in the 1920 general election. The Republicans took 404 of the 531 electoral votes, the largest margin in one hundred years. Roosevelt himself had expected the outcome. His mother wrote in her diary that he seemed "rather relieved not to be elected."

While that probably wasn't true, Roosevelt was ready to return to private life. Besides practicing law, he went to work for a company that issued bonds. Roosevelt did not give up politics completely, but the progressive reformer had rejoined the ranks of conservative businessmen.

Franklin, shown here with Eleanor, maintained an active lifestyle during his summers at Campobello, swimming and sailing with friends and family.

CHAPTER THREE

CRIPPLED

"I don't know what is the matter with me,
Louis, I just don't know."
—Franklin D. Roosevelt to Louis Howe immediately
after being struck with paralysis

Franklin scanned the horizon from the deck of his twenty-four-foot sloop. He and three of his five children were sailing in the clear waters off Maine, a short distance from his family's summer home at Campobello. He'd joined them here just a few days before, escaping New York City and work. Though his right leg bothered him and he felt tired, he hoped the sea would invigorate him.

As they sailed, someone in the boat noticed smoke curling in the distance. They found a fire raging on a small island. Franklin and the children worked for hours beating out the flames with evergreen branches. When they brought the flames under control, Franklin led them on a two-mile run, capped off by a plunge into the icy Atlantic.

The chilly water always lifted his spirits, but it didn't work on that particular day. "I didn't get the usual revitalization, the glow I'd expected," he remembered later. "When I reached the house . . . I sat reading for a while, too tired even to dress. I'd never felt quite that way before." Finally he told the others he was tired and had a touch of lumbago, a term used at the time to describe a painful backache. He climbed up the stairs to bed. Those steps on August 10, 1921, were the last he would ever take on his own.

POLIO

No one knew that Franklin had contracted poliomyelitis, a disease commonly known as polio. "I first had a chill in the evening which lasted practically all night," Roosevelt later told a doctor. "The following morning the muscles of the right knee appeared weak and by afternoon I was unable to support my weight on my right leg. That evening the left knee began to weaken also and by the following morning I was unable to stand up. This was accompanied by a continuing temperature of about 102 and I felt thoroughly achy all over. By the end of the third day practically all muscles from the chest down were involved. Above the chest the only symptom was a weakening of the two large thumb muscles making it impossible to write."

Two weeks passed before a doctor realized Franklin had polio. There was little to be done but make him comfortable. Eleanor nursed him through the "trial by fire" with help from Louis Howe. Franklin's high fever made him delirious at times. He was in bed for a month before he could be moved to New York. "I felt God had abandoned me," Franklin later told a friend.

DID PARALYSIS HELP FDR?

Historians have raised interesting questions about Roosevelt's paralysis: Did it change his personality? Did it make him a better president? Some believe that it did. Perhaps, they say, it made him more aware of the suffering of others. Eleanor claimed that his disease "gave him strength and courage he had not had before."

Others disagree. Roosevelt had already shown great ability and optimism. "Throughout his adult life," points out his son Elliott, "his was the same personality, the mixture, as perhaps his most observant biographer [James MacGregor Burns] noted, of lion and fox."

Another Roosevelt biographer, Kenneth A. Davis, believes that in some ways Roosevelt's paralysis gave him an advantage. "It commonly made . . . others want . . . to please, emulate, and if at all possible, agree with this man who demonstrated so much courage, strength of character, and optimistic confidence . . . under pressures that would have crushed an ordinary mortal into chronic depression and resentful dependency." And, Davis notes, though Franklin might have been "known to be crippled, he was not *felt* to be so."

✧ ──────────

Franklin tried to conceal his paralysis, rarely allowing his photo to be taken while in a wheelchair. This is one of only a few such images.

HIDDEN AWAY

When reporters heard rumors that Roosevelt was sick, they tried to check them out. Howe realized that even if the paralysis was only temporary, news about it might kill Roosevelt's career. In those days, someone with a physical disability was often considered mentally deficient as well. The disabled were hidden away. They rarely worked and almost never held political office. Hoping to salvage the situation, Howe lied about how bad the illness was.

It is unclear when Roosevelt realized he would never walk again. In fact, he may not have admitted it to himself for many years. Throughout the 1920s, he talked of full recovery. He swam and exercised and tried every suggestion to get better. "It seemed constantly to be 'another two years,'" said his son Elliott.

Displeased with the wheelchairs of the day, Franklin designed his own from kitchen chairs. On his feet and lower body, he wore a set of thick braces, which kept his legs straight. A screw at the knee worked as a hinge, allowing him to bend his

✧ ————————

During the mid-1920s, Franklin began visiting a resort in Warm Springs, Georgia. He felt that swimming in the hot springs there improved the condition of his legs.

leg to sit. The braces were cumbersome, but they made it possible to stand. They also made it easier to maneuver with crutches.

Eventually Roosevelt developed a way of moving with the help of one other person that made it seem as if he were walking alone. He first perfected the method with Elliott when his son was eighteen. Elliott held his own right arm stiff, almost like a guardrail. Franklin gripped it with his left hand. In his right, he held a cane. He shifted his weight from one side to another, using his powerful trunk muscles to pull up his legs as he moved forward. With his constant smile and seemingly casual conversation,

—————————— ◇ ——————————

Franklin taught himself to stand. Here, he supports himself with a cane, leg braces, and the arm of his son John.

Franklin diverted attention from his uncertain gait. He couldn't go very far or very fast, but he did seem to walk.

COMMITMENT TO POLITICS

Meanwhile, Roosevelt nourished his dream of returning to politics. He and Eleanor worked to support other Democrats. Though they remained important figures behind the scenes, Franklin wasn't content. Despite his disability, he had not given up his dream of becoming president, but he quickly realized just how difficult it would be.

———————————————— ◇ ————————————————

In the years after Franklin contracted polio, Eleanor (right) *became more and more interested in politics.*

*Franklin found ways to continue doing the outdoor activities
he enjoyed, such as fishing.*

———————————— ✧ ————————————

After Franklin had recovered from the early stages of
polio, he started going to dinner parties again. At one
party, he crawled from the dining room to the living room
after dinner. For Franklin, this seemed natural. He did it at
home all the time, but it disturbed others. His host was
overcome with pity, even though greatly impressed by
Franklin's courage. Roosevelt realized that no one votes for
someone they pity. He knew that if he was going to run
for office, he had to walk, not crawl. He had to do what-
ever was needed to appear robust.

Gradually, he learned to stand for hours when it would
have been more comfortable to sit. He learned to smile
despite the pain. He learned to do things that emphasized

his vigor. He learned how to make his halting walk seem steadier than it really was. He made it look as if he could truly walk on his own, instead of relying on someone else's arm to hold him up. He found situations, such as campaigning from convertible cars, in which his disability wouldn't be noticed. He began forbidding photographs that showed him in a wheelchair or even revealed his braces. If the common image of a disabled person was someone who was weak, stupid, or depressed, Franklin was exactly the opposite. He was a fighter—full of life, with plenty of energy and a smile for nearly everyone.

CHAPTER FOUR

AMERICA'S PATHFINDER

*"There had been a plowing up of his nature.
The man emerged completely warm hearted,
with new humility of spirit and a firmer
understanding of philosophical concepts."*
—Frances Perkins, cabinet member and friend of
Roosevelt, talking about the effects of polio on
Roosevelt's political career

On June 27, 1928, Franklin Delano Roosevelt stood in the sweltering heat of Houston, Texas, his son Elliott at his side. Roosevelt was about to make the most important speech of his life. Before he could do so, however, he had to take four more steps.

Roosevelt had come to the Democratic National Convention to nominate New York governor Al Smith for president, as he had done four years earlier in Madison Square Garden in New York. Fifteen thousand spectators were packed into the hall. Perhaps fifteen million more were listening at home on radios. If Roosevelt did well, his dream of returning to national politics might be fulfilled. If he gave a bad speech—or much worse, if he fell before he made it to the microphone—his career would be over.

Four more steps. Roosevelt smiled and waved despite the strain of the heavy braces, despite the sweat rolling from his brow and down his back. He pivoted on Elliott's arm. Once, twice, three more times. Franklin made it.

The crowd roared. He waved his hands and told the convention delegates that the president had to have a "quality of soul which makes him a strong help to those in sorrow or trouble, that quality which makes him not merely

————————————— ✧ —————————————

Franklin appears with John Davis (middle), a prominent Democratic politician, and Al Smith (right).

admired, but loved by all the people—the quality of sympathetic understanding of the human heart, of real interest in one's fellow man. . . .

"America needs," Roosevelt continued, "a pathfinder, a blazer of the trail to the high road that will avoid the bottomless morass of crass materialism that has engulfed so many great civilizations of the past."

Smith won the nomination, and Roosevelt stepped back on stage. He had done almost too well. Everyone wanted him to run for governor of New York—everyone but Roosevelt's closest advisers and Franklin Roosevelt himself.

RUNNING FOR GOVERNOR

In the summer of 1928, it looked like the Republicans would stay in power for years. Like many people, Franklin believed Smith would lose his bid for the presidency to Republican Herbert Hoover. Franklin thought the Republicans would also sweep the governor's race and many others. "Every war brings after it a period of materialism and conservatism," Roosevelt told a friend. "The people will not turn out the Republicans while wages are good and the markets are booming." He said the nation wouldn't elect a Democratic president "until the Republicans had led us into a serious period of depression and unemployment."

The only family member who seemed definitely to want Franklin to run for office was his daughter, Anna, who sent him a telegram with the words "Go ahead and take it." He wired her back, "You ought to be spanked."

Still, Roosevelt must have been tempted as pressure mounted. Surely he would lose. He and Howe had gone over the odds a million times. But what if he tried really hard? What if he approached the campaign the way he tackled everything else? Wouldn't he win? How could he lose?

Eleanor later claimed that she "did not want him to do it." Nevertheless she let Al Smith talk her into calling Franklin at Warm Springs, a resort in Georgia that he had purchased in 1926 because of its warm, soothing pools of mineral water. Franklin was avoiding calls—but not calls from Eleanor. When he came to the phone, she handed it to Smith, who pleaded with him to run. Roosevelt finally gave in.

AN "UNFAIR" CANDIDACY

The Republicans used Roosevelt's polio as a campaign issue. Newspapers also used it, saying that the nomination was "unfair" to Roosevelt because he was disabled. They implied he was weak, sick, and incompetent because of his difficulties walking.

"Frank Roosevelt today is mentally as good as he ever was in his life," responded Smith. "Physically he is as good as he ever was in his life. His whole trouble is his lack of muscular control of his lower limbs. But the answer to that is that a governor does not have to be an acrobat." As Smith pointed out, "ninety-five percent" of the governor's job was done sitting at a desk.

Roosevelt made a joke of his disability. He said he couldn't run the way most politicians did—he'd have to walk into office. He campaigned throughout upstate New York in his convertible. He appeared active and vigorous.

Still, it was a tough year for Democrats. The Republicans reminded voters of the current prosperity with the slogan, "A chicken in every pot and a car in every garage."

ROOSEVELT'S CARS

Franklin Roosevelt first won election to the New York State Senate in 1910 with a major innovation—he drove around his district in a car. He loved the freedom of movement automobiles allowed, and he valued them even more after he was paralyzed.

Roosevelt had a series of autos adapted so he could drive them even though his legs were paralyzed. A long rod at the left side of the car allowed him to depress the clutch while changing gears. Another on the right side controlled the gas pedal.

Even as president, Roosevelt often drove when he returned to Hyde Park. He and his cars were a common sight in the Hudson Valley near his estate. Roosevelt's 1936 Ford Phaeton is still on display at the FDR Library and Museum in Hyde Park.

Roosevelt greets supporters from his car in Warm Springs, Georgia.

*Hoover served as U.S. secretary of
commerce during the prosperous 1920s.*

——————— ✧ ———————

Republican presidential candidate Herbert Hoover declared,
"We in America today are nearer to the final triumph over
poverty than ever before in the history of any land. The
poorhouse is vanishing from among us."

'TIL THE END

As the first returns came in on election night, it was clear
Hoover had defeated Smith. Roosevelt was also doing poor-
ly, dragged down by Smith's defeat. In those days, it usually took many hours and, in some cases, days to count all
the ballots. Smith's defeat was so overwhelming that the
early editions of the newspapers declared the race over and
said Roosevelt had lost, too.

"We'll stay around until it is over," Roosevelt told his aides stubbornly at his headquarters in the Biltmore Hotel in New York City. Slowly, the numbers from the small upstate rural counties made their way in. These areas always voted heavily for Republicans—except in this election. When all of the votes were added up, they showed a big surprise. In a Republican year, Democrat Franklin Delano Roosevelt had won the governorship by a margin of 25,564 votes. The margin was tight, given that more than 4,000,000 votes had been cast, but a victory was a victory.

ELEANOR AS ENVOY

After Franklin became physically impaired, his political career depended more than ever on help from Louis Howe and Eleanor. Roosevelt had always depended on Howe for his insight and hard work. Eleanor's involvement was new. She helped her husband as an envoy, or representative. After he was elected, this role expanded and became critical.

Eleanor had many teachers and helpers, but Louis and Franklin were the most important. Louis taught her how to speak in public. He changed her "from a nervous introvert into an outgoing political being," said her son Elliott. Howe reviewed her appearances and worked relentlessly to eliminate the nervous giggle that marred her speeches. He got Eleanor involved in the women's division of the Democratic state committee and had her raise money for the party, which increased her power and influence.

From her husband, Eleanor learned to see beyond the smiling faces of the officials greeting her. "At first my reports were highly unsatisfactory to him," Eleanor recalled in one of her autobiographies, *This I Remember.* "I would tell him what was on the menu for the day and he would ask: 'Did you look to see whether the inmates actually were getting that food?' I learned to look into the cooking pots on the stove and to find out if the contents corresponded to the menu; I learned to notice whether the beds were too close together, and whether they were folded up and put in closets behind doors during the day, which would indicate that they filled the corridors at night; I learned to watch the patients' attitude towards the staff."

Many people said that Eleanor became Franklin's legs, going places that he couldn't go. He called her his conscience. She was also a constant adviser, a deputy speaker, and a tireless fund-raiser. They worked as a team and enhanced Roosevelt's career. In some ways, this team could reach even further than Franklin alone could have before he was stricken with polio.

LIFE IN ALBANY

When Smith encouraged Roosevelt to run for governor, he may have thought Franklin could be easily controlled. Smith urged Roosevelt to reappoint several people who had worked for him as governor. Franklin, however, quickly brought in his own people and followed his own course. After a slow start with the conservative legislature, Roosevelt began to win support. He issued press releases, made regular radio addresses, and toured upstate by barge along the old Erie Canal.

Farm reform was one of Roosevelt's main issues during the 1928 campaign. Like farmers elsewhere, New York farmers were hurt by high taxes, low prices for crops, and the changing nature of agriculture. After Roosevelt was elected, he sought to help them. Aided by people such as Henry Morgenthau Jr., a friend who edited the *American Agriculturist* periodical, Roosevelt passed tax relief measures to lower farmers' costs. The real effect of Roosevelt's governorship, however, wasn't seen until the stock market crashed in October 1929. Banks closed overnight, businesses went bust, and thousands of people lost their jobs. The decade of prosperity Americans had enjoyed ended with a bang.

This autographed photo shows Governor Roosevelt at work in Albany.
He became popular with New Yorkers for his economic relief efforts.

CHAPTER FIVE

THE GREAT DEPRESSION

*"I assert that modern society, acting through its
government, owes the definite obligation to
prevent the starvation or the dire want of any
of its fellow men and women who try to
maintain themselves but cannot."*

—Franklin D. Roosevelt

Like other government leaders, Governor Roosevelt moved
slowly in the months after the stock market crash. He
increased state jobs programs and pushed his farming
reforms. This helped, but only a little.

Roosevelt kept looking for fresh solutions to the growing crisis. Eventually, he began a program called the
Temporary Emergency Relief Administration (TERA). This
program provided an average of twenty-three dollars a
month to needy families. Not all of Roosevelt's solutions
involved the government. For example, he asked businesses
to change their production schedules to help avoid seasonal

unemployment. But Roosevelt's massive government-spon-
sored relief programs were a major break with the past.

REELECTION LANDSLIDE—AND BEYOND

Just as voters gave Republicans credit for the good times,
they blamed them for the bad. When Herbert Hoover had
won the election, he personified a government that brought
prosperity. After the Great Depression hit, he symbolized a
government that refused to help people despite their great
suffering. He seemed cold and heartless.

When Roosevelt ran for reelection as governor in 1930,
the election quickly became a referendum on the role of
government. Hoover sent three members of his cabinet to
New York to campaign against Roosevelt. They tried to
divert attention from the economy by calling attention to
corruption in New York City.

Franklin fought back hard. He told a Democratic friend
in Pennsylvania, "If any of your friends ask about the New
York situation, tell them it is all right and that we are
throwing the burden on the Republicans." Roosevelt blamed
speculation and greed for the Great Depression, not Hoover.
But, referring to President Hoover, Roosevelt also said, "If
Washington had the courage to apply the brakes . . . the fall
from the heights would not have been so appallingly great."

Roosevelt's reelection victory was the greatest landslide
in New York State history. The people wanted the government to do something.

"FORGOTTEN MAN"

"The Democrats nominated their president yesterday,"
joked nationally known commentator Will Rogers after

Franklin was reelected. As the depression continued, the joke seemed more and more likely to become reality. Roosevelt's willingness to experiment, as well as his reputation as a fighter, made him an obvious choice.

The economic situation in the country steadily worsened. While estimates vary, most historians believe that about one third of the country's workers were unemployed at the height of the Great Depression in 1932. Many of those who had jobs weren't making enough money to get by. In New York, roughly 10 percent of the state's residents received TERA grants by the winter of 1931–1932.

———————————— ✧ ————————————

Large groups of out-of-work Americans lined up at employment agencies during the early 1930s.

Governor Roosevelt continued his experiments, sometimes moving boldly, more often cautiously, as the 1932 presidential election neared.

When Roosevelt decided to seek his party's nomination, he declared that the government must help the "forgotten man"—people in the middle and lower classes. Roosevelt suggested that the federal government help farmers and

———————————— ✧ ————————————

Eleanor and Franklin campaigned together, often from trains. Here, they do some early campaigning for president in 1932.

homeowners with mortgages if necessary. His program for the nation extended some of the ideas tried in New York. It also included payments to people who were out of work, government-funded work projects, more regulation of the stock market, and changes in banking. He also supported programs to protect the environment.

"STOP ROOSEVELT"

Many rich people reacted strongly when Roosevelt said he would help "the forgotten man." They interpreted this as an attack on the rich, especially since Roosevelt blamed the Great Depression on abuses by the rich and on the imbalance of wealth in the United States. One of his cousins, Mary W. Roosevelt, called his attitude "silly." There were no forgotten men, she said, "but plenty of them [people] who thought they were owed something for nothing." To many wealthy people, Roosevelt was a traitor to his social class.

Roosevelt's Democratic political opponents tried to "Stop Roosevelt" from getting the nomination. Delegates to the national convention choose presidential candidates. Roosevelt gathered a majority of delegates before the 1932 convention, but he couldn't quite amass the two-thirds needed to win under party rules. The Stop Roosevelt strategy was simple. If the opposition could hold together through the first several votes, a compromise candidate would have to be found. This had worked in earlier conventions. The fact that it had not given the Democrats a strong candidate didn't seem to bother those opposing Roosevelt. Many thought that *any* Democrat could beat Hoover—and they were probably right.

When the convention met in Chicago Stadium at the end of June, Roosevelt made phone calls from Albany. By custom, candidates never attended the convention. They had to appear above politics and reluctant to run, even though the reality was very different. Roosevelt's friends, including Louis Howe and Jim Farley (another political ally from New York), had been working in Chicago for more than a week. They had performed "jujitsu" (an intricate art of weaponless fighting) said one historian, rounding up votes for Roosevelt. But they still had not been able to cinch a win.

Roosevelt listened to reports all Thursday night, June 30, as the candidates were nominated. He told Farley to move for a vote, even though they knew they didn't have two-thirds of the votes. Delaying might make them seem weak.

Roosevelt won 666 ½ votes—464 ½ more than his nearest rival, but not enough to win. Two more ballots inched the total higher, but not enough. When the delegates went home at 9:15 A.M. on Friday, some thought Roosevelt had been stopped.

Farley and Howe worked furiously. They persuaded Texan John Nance Garner to drop his candidacy in exchange for being named vice president. Garner's switch did the trick. Roosevelt listened by phone Friday night as the crowd celebrated his victory. As soon as he put down the phone, the governor launched into a plan that would dramatize how active and different his campaign would be.

"THIS CRUSADE"

Early Saturday morning, Franklin, Eleanor, Elliott, and a host of assistants piled into two limousines. With a police escort, they sped through Albany to the nearby airfield, where they boarded a chartered Ford Tri-Motor plane. It took off into turbulent air, bumping along so severely that everyone except Franklin and Elliott got sick.

Eleanor sat quietly in her seat—and not just because her stomach felt queasy. She didn't want her husband to be president. She knew what the strain would mean, for him and for her. She consoled herself with the idea that her husband's religious beliefs had given him confidence and a sense of obligation. "He felt that human beings were given tasks to perform and with those tasks the ability and strength to put them through. He could pray for help and guidance and have faith in his own judgment as a result."

Franklin was excited. His flight to Chicago to accept the nomination was a stroke of genius. "He knew that smashing precedent by accepting on the spot, he could thrill the voters with a sense of decisive leadership," said Elliott.

Thousands of people mobbed the plane when it landed. As the travelers climbed into cars that would take them to the convention, Louis Howe shoved a speech into Franklin's hand, telling him it was far better than the one Franklin planned to give. Roosevelt, smiling for the crowd, spoke to Howe out of the corner of his mouth. "Damn it, Louis, I'm the nominee." He waited until he had arrived at the convention and reached the podium and then looked it over. Howe's speech *was* good. He stitched the two speeches together on the spot.

"I pledge you, I pledge myself to a new deal for the American people," he told the audience, promising not only to get the nation back on its feet but to distribute its great wealth more equally among all people. "Give me your

Roosevelt delivers a rousing acceptance speech at the 1932
Democratic National Convention in Chicago, where he announced
a New Deal for the American people.

help, not to win votes alone, but to win in this crusade for the American people!" The crowd went wild. "New Deal" became Roosevelt's rallying cry.

Roosevelt crushed Herbert Hoover that November, garnering 22,800,000 votes to Hoover's 15,750,000. When the returns came in, he held his sobbing mother tightly and told her it was the "greatest night of my life."

CHAPTER SIX

A NEW DEAL

"The only thing we have to fear is fear itself."
—Franklin D. Roosevelt, First Inaugural Address

Bareheaded despite the cold weather, on March 4, 1933, Franklin Delano Roosevelt leaned on his son James as he walked stiff-legged toward the front of the stage set outside the Capitol in Washington, D.C. Thousands of spectators craned to catch a view as Franklin put his hand on the family Bible. His fingers rested on the thirteenth verse of the thirteenth chapter of Paul's First Epistle to the Corinthians: "And now abideth faith, hope, charity, these three; but the greatest of these is charity."

After he took the oath of office, Roosevelt gripped the lectern firmly with both hands and began his speech. "I am sure that my fellow Americans expect that on my induction into the Presidency I will address them with a candor and a decision which the present situation of our Nation impels," he began. "This is preeminently the time to speak the

Roosevelt and Eleanor ride through Washington on inauguration day.

———————————— ✧ ————————————

truth." The words hung in the air. Then the optimist who had kept up his spirits through his long struggle with polio declared, "So first of all, let me assert my firm belief that the only thing we have to fear is fear itself—nameless, unreasoning, unjustified terror which paralyzes needed efforts to convert retreat into advance."

In the space of thirty-three words, Franklin D. Roosevelt sounded the trumpet for a charge against the depression. He continued with a thunderous image of righteousness from the Bible—appropriate, since he had written a draft of the speech while sitting in St. James Church back at Hyde Park. It was a place he often went to collect his thoughts and renew his spirit. "The money changers have fled from their high seats in the temple of our civilization. We may now restore that temple to the ancient truths."

He continued, "We do not distrust the future of essential democracy," said Roosevelt. "The people of the United States have not failed. In their need they have registered a mandate that they want direct, vigorous action. They have asked for discipline and direction under leadership. They have made me the present instrument of their wishes. In the spirit of the gift, I take it."

THE BANKS

While Roosevelt delivered his speech, his advisers worked with bankers on a plan to solve the country's banking crisis. For several weeks, panics, or runs, on banks had wracked the country. Anxious people went to banks and tried to withdraw all their money. Since their money was not physically in the banks—it had been loaned to others—this caused serious shortfalls. There just wasn't enough cash on hand. When too many people tried to withdraw their money from a bank, the bank failed. When a bank failed, the depositors lost all their money. That caused more runs on other banks, as people lost confidence and worried that they, too, would lose their savings. "Something close to six million depositors, or one family in every four, lost their savings (for many, their life savings) in the bank failures of 1929–33," according to an expert on the crisis.

In one of Roosevelt's first acts as president, he declared a national bank holiday. This closed all the banks in the country and gave him time to present a solution to

Nervous crowds gathered in front of banks, as people clamored to withdraw their money before the banks became unable to pay.

——————————————— ✧ ———————————————

Congress. At the same time, Roosevelt reassured people that the problem would be solved.

"My friends, I want to talk for a few minutes with the people of the United States about banking," he said in a nationally broadcast radio show on March 12, 1933. "To talk with the comparatively few who understand the mechanics of banking, but more particularly with the over-whelming majority of you who use banks for the making of deposits and the drawing of checks. I want to tell you what has been done in the last few days, and why it was done, and what the next steps are going to be."

This direct address to the American public was unprecedented. Roosevelt took a complicated issue and explained it in a way everyone could understand. His radio addresses continued and soon became known as "fireside chats."

CONSERVATIVE MOVES

Roosevelt's new banking laws were passed quickly. Among other things, they called for a federal review of banks and the use of Federal Reserve notes for cash. These reforms were conservative. In fact, they were similar to proposals Hoover's advisers had made. There had been calls for much more radical action. Even many bankers wanted the federal government to take over the banking system—to "nationalize" the banks. Roosevelt disagreed. He even hesitated to insure bank deposits, thinking that measure was too radical. (A few months later, in June 1933, he agreed to federal insurance for bank deposits. That measure is considered one of the foundations of the American banking system.)

Roosevelt's actions in the banking crisis were similar to his methods when dealing with many of the problems his administration faced. They seem a reflection of his personality. Even though he was open to new ideas, he moved cautiously at first, just as he had done as governor. He changed his methods until he solved the problem, just as he had done when trying to walk again. Franklin also tended to make sure he had voters' backing before acting. While he worked constantly to spread his views, rarely did he go further than he judged the public as a whole would accept.

A RUSH OF ACTIVITY

Proposals to deal with the country's various problems poured out of the White House. At the same time, Congress pushed its own ideas. In different cases, such as insuring bank deposits, Roosevelt went along with Congress although he didn't completely agree.

"The thing to do was strike while Congress was hot," Roosevelt told one of his close advisers, Ray Moley. The first one hundred days of his administration saw the passage of fifteen major bills. Besides banking legislation, the measures included the Farm Credit Administration (FCA), the National Recovery Act (NRA), the Civil Conservation Corps (CCC), and a variety of work programs. Congress's

———————————————— ✧ ————————————————

Roosevelt visits a Civil Conservation Corps (CCC) camp in Virginia. The CCC provided training and work for about 2.5 million jobless men.

output during this period still remains a record.

Production in the country's factories and on its farms did not snap back to the level of the 1920s, but people clearly felt more optimistic and more hopeful as the New Deal went on. Most importantly, the country's economic and political systems had been saved.

AN EASYGOING DAD

One day a collect call came into the White House. The operator put it through because it was President Roosevelt's son Elliott.

"How are you, Bunny?" asked Franklin, picking up the phone.

Actually, Elliott told his dad, he was just about out of money and stuck in Little Rock, Arkansas. Married only the year before, Elliott had already fallen out of love with his wife. He was traveling to California where he might take a job with an airline company—or might not. Still in his early twenties, Elliott was fleeing a life of responsibility. He wanted to know if his father could lend him some cash.

"How much money do you have?" Franklin asked.

"Thirty dollars," said Elliott.

The president reached into his own pocket.

"I have only eight dollars myself," he told his son. "And I've just shut down the banks. I suggest you stop at some prosperous farmer's house and perhaps earn enough money to continue your trip."

Franklin's advice was typical of his relationship with his children. He rarely scolded them, preferring gentle humor. When the children were young, Franklin had never liked to discipline them. Now that they were grown, he might threaten to punish them by refusing to invite them to family gatherings, but even then, he would inevitably relent.

AT HOME IN THE WHITE HOUSE

As president, Franklin quickly established a daily routine. He awoke by 8:30 A.M., had breakfast, and read a few newspapers. According to Eleanor, only his grandchildren were allowed to disturb him early in the morning, although his door was never locked. His secretary Marguerite "Missy" LeHand and Louis Howe both lived in the White House. They generally came in while he ate or read the papers. By 10 A.M., Franklin had been dressed and then wheeled to the

———————————— ◇ ————————————

Roosevelt conducts business in his formal work space, the Oval Office.

White House elevator. Usually his business took him to the Oval Office. Twice a week, he held press conferences, and every Friday there were cabinet meetings. Every day around 5:00 P.M., he retreated upstairs for "children's hour." Cocktails were generally served, and staff and friends could share gossip. Business talk was off-limits.

The Roosevelts installed what Eleanor called "sturdy furniture" in the White House. Eleanor replaced priceless antiques that she feared might be broken by her "husky sons" and by the dozens of assistants the Roosevelts gathered around them. Except for state dinners, the family paid for their own food and that of their helpers and guests.

The president often conducted meetings in his upstairs study after dinner, but he also relaxed with movies. He loved comedies and avoided dramas whenever possible. And "he always had a Mickey Mouse" cartoon, according to Eleanor.

ELEANOR'S ROLE

Shortly after the 1933 inauguration, Eleanor had asked Franklin if she could be his secretary. Missy had worked as his secretary for years, so Franklin told Eleanor that giving her that job might upset Missy. In some ways, he felt more comfortable with Missy than with Eleanor. He joked and shared stories with Missy that he would never tell his wife. Eleanor herself realized she was sometimes acting as "a spoil sport and policeman."

Eleanor gradually found her role as an advocate for public housing and other assistance to help the poor. Refusing to go along with discrimination toward African Americans, she often visited black institutions and attended events where she was one of the few invited whites. Traveling widely across the country, Eleanor became an unofficial spokesperson for the New Deal. Eventually she wrote a widely circulated newspaper column called "My Day." Franklin and many others called her "the conscience of the New Deal."

CHAPTER SEVEN

SECURITY AND DEMOCRACY

"It is time for all Americans, Americans of all the Americas, to stop being deluded by the romantic notion that the Americans can go on living happily and peacefully in a Nazi-dominated world."

—Franklin D. Roosevelt

Franklin Roosevelt drew himself up behind his Oval Office desk. He leaned back against the green swivel chair, arms on the rests. The Democratic congressmen sitting across from him this wintry day in early March 1935 had come with bad news—the plan to give pensions to the elderly had fizzled.

Roosevelt's popularity with the people was still strong, but his influence in Congress had dropped. His aides gave him conflicting advice about the depression. One said the country would soon be back on its feet. Another said the New Deal hadn't even made an impact yet.

The president leaned forward as the congressmen paused. Sometimes he felt like a prisoner behind his desk, unable to get up and walk out when he wanted. But Franklin was always stubborn and determined when attacked. Once he made up his mind, he did not retreat.

Franklin raised his chin slightly, then pursed his lips. It was a trademark Roosevelt pose. Old-age insurance, he told his visitors sharply, was the heart of his Social Security plan. It was as important as unemployment insurance and relief for the extremely poor. They must fight for it, and it would pass. All of it—together.

SOCIAL SECURITY

People had been trying to get old-age pensions and insurance to help the unemployed long before the Great Depression. Many European countries had such programs, but American politicians had long opposed them. They believed such programs "'sapped' the 'initiative' and destroyed the 'moral fiber' of the helped individual." Roosevelt realized that many of the elderly had been poor even during the boom times. He saw unemployment as a problem for all of society. Even if the depression were to end abruptly, these problems needed a long-lasting solution. His solution included three main ideas:

- Unemployment payments should be insurance, not a "dole" or handout. There should be no shame in receiving them.
- The old-age program should be "pay as you go." In other words, it would be financed from present contributions or taxes.
- Support for poor families and children—known

eventually as welfare—should be paid by grants to the states, which would administer the funds.

"No one can guarantee this country against the dangers of future depressions but we can reduce these dangers," Roosevelt told Congress, explaining his ideas. "We can eliminate many of the factors that cause economic depression, and we can provide the means of mitigating their results. This plan for economic security is at once a measure of prevention and a method of alleviation [relief]."

There was much opposition, especially to the pension plan. Speaking for many in the country, the head of the American Bar Association (a lawyers' organization) declared that guaranteeing to help people in their old age "sooner or later will bring about the inevitable abandonment of private capitalism." When they met with Roosevelt in March, supporters of the bill were ready to give up on old-age pensions. Passing laws for unemployment insurance and welfare seemed the best they could do. But Roosevelt persisted. Finally, he got most of what he wanted and signed the Social Security Act of 1935 into law on August 14, 1935.

——————————— ✧
Unemployed men sign up for economic assistance from the government.

Historians point out that the bill was a "hodgepodge." It paid relatively small pensions and failed to provide relief for many who desperately needed it. However, it represented a turning point in American history. The bill was gradually expanded and improved. The retirement programs in Social Security still remain in effect, as do unemployment insurance and welfare.

ROOSEVELT AS POLITICIAN

As the worst of the depression lifted, more politicians and businessmen started to criticize Roosevelt. A few wanted him to move faster with promised reforms. Many others thought he was moving too fast and claimed that he was leading the country toward communism. Through it all, Roosevelt remained popular with the voters because of his policies and his positive, fighting attitude.

Besides using radio addresses, the president used press conferences and interviews with reporters to make his views known. With a wide command of facts and a teasing sense of humor, Roosevelt handled the press easily. Even though he felt the newspapers distorted his statements, much of his message got through to the people. While he did not compromise on his major goals, he often compromised with Congress to get what he wanted. He used patronage, the promise of jobs, as a trading weapon with congressmen. On a personal level, Roosevelt could charm nearly anyone.

REELECTED

When Roosevelt decided to run for reelection in 1936, attacks by the rich and by Republicans gave him easy ammunition. People who had suffered during the Great

*When Roosevelt wanted to deliver a message to the American people
that was not influenced by the press, he gave a radio address.*

───────────── ✧ ─────────────

Depression saw the wealthy as their enemies. "The hatred
of the rich," notes historian Arthur Schlesinger Jr., "had
transformed him [Roosevelt] into a national hero."

"In 1932, the issue was the restoration of American
democracy, and the American people were in a mood to
win," Roosevelt said during a campaign speech at Madison
Square Garden in New York City just before the 1936 election. "They did win. In 1936 the issue is the preservation
of their victory."

As the crowd continued to cheer, Roosevelt cited the

New Deal programs that had put the country back on its feet. But he added that "business and financial monopoly" were trying to regain power. "Never before in all our history have these forces been so united against one candidate as they stand today. They are unanimous in their hate for me—and I welcome their hatred!" Roosevelt found it difficult to speak over the applause.

"We have only just begun to fight," he said finally. "The recovery we are winning is more than economic. In it are included justice and love and humility, not for ourselves as individuals alone, but for our nation." A few days later, the people gave Roosevelt 27,751,597 votes to his opponent's 16,679,583. But the attacks on the New Deal had just begun.

PACKING THE COURT

In May 1935, the U.S. Supreme Court struck down much of the legislation organizing the National Recovery Act (NRA), saying it was unconstitutional. On January 6, 1936, the Court ruled that the Agricultural Adjustment Administration (AAA), created in 1933 to raise farm prices by limiting production, was also illegal. Over the course of several months, the justices, the majority of whom were conservative, gutted much of the early New Deal legislation.

Roosevelt fought back in a number of ways. He pushed for new legislation that would stand up to the legal challenges, and he criticized the Court.

He also attempted to add more justices to the Court. Roosevelt claimed this was simply to help the older judges with a heavy workload, but it was clear that he wanted men who would be friendlier to his programs. "The courts . . .

have cast doubts on the ability of the elected Congress to protect us against catastrophe," Roosevelt told the nation in his March 9, 1937, fireside chat. The Supreme Court, he said, had gone beyond its powers by judging whether or not a law was constitutional. "The Court . . . has improperly set itself up as a third house of the Congress . . . reading into the Constitution words and implications which are not there, and which were never intended to be there. We . . . have, therefore, reached the point as a nation where we must take action to save the Constitution from the Court and the Court from itself."

Roosevelt's proposal was seen as interference with the balance of power. It was called "packing the court" and quickly denounced. He was forced to back down. At the same time, however, the Court began ruling in favor of major New Deal legislation, including Social Security. As the older justices retired, Roosevelt appointed replacements who would side with him. Even so, the president had lost some prestige, and the momentum of many New Deal programs stalled during the fight.

GATHERING STORM

While the United States struggled through the 1930s, Europe and Asia were roiled by war. Japan had invaded the Manchurian region of China in 1931, beginning a campaign of aggression in Asia. Hamstrung by the depression, the American response under Hoover and then Roosevelt was weak. Both presidents hesitated to impose economic sanctions, such as banning the sale of oil or other goods. Roosevelt told his cabinet shortly after coming into office that the United States must "avoid war with Japan."

SAVE AMERICA FIRST!

This 1930s cartoon shows that many Americans felt their country faced too many domestic problems to be concerned with European politics.

———————————— ✧ ————————————

In Europe both Italy and Germany were well on their way to war. In 1935 Italy had invaded Ethiopia, one of the few independent countries in Africa. German troops marched into Austria in March 1938. Six months later, Great Britain and France allowed German leader Adolf Hitler to seize a large portion of Czechoslovakia called

Sudentenland. Roosevelt realized that Hitler had to be met with force, or at least the threat of force, but the public was overwhelmingly against U.S. involvement.

Speaking about Congress's Neutrality Act in 1935, Roosevelt told his ambassador to Germany that he was trying to persuade Congress to give him more leeway in the event of conflict. He still hoped the country could remain neutral. "I do not know that the United States can save civilization but at least by our example we can make people think and give them the opportunity of saving themselves. The trouble is that the people of Germany, Italy and Japan are not given the privilege of thinking."

The German invasion of Poland in September 1939 ended any possibility of peace. In the spring of 1940, German troops blitzed through France, quickly overwhelming the defenses. Bombers ravaged England. With the Soviet Union aligned with Germany, the days of democracy in Europe seemed numbered.

A THIRD TERM

In a note to Eleanor in August 1938, Franklin warned her to "have no discussion of a third term" at a forum she was attending. Eleanor wrote back that a friend "wants you for a third term and I thought this most unwise. You know I do not believe in it."

The U.S. Constitution put no limit on the number of terms a president could serve. But ever since George Washington, American presidents had limited themselves to two terms. Roosevelt seemed ready to follow that tradition. Though he made no public commitment, privately his decision seemed to have been made. "I am tied down to this chair day after day, week after week, and month after month," he told Senator George Norris of Nebraska in February. "And I can't stand it any longer. I can't go on with it." Eleanor was convinced he would retire. "There were innumerable things that all his life he had meant to do—write on naval subjects, go through his papers, letters, and so on," she said. Franklin had even agreed on a job at Vassar College near his home in Hyde Park.

When war exploded in Europe, however, Roosevelt's supporters pressured him to run. They wanted a strong leader to prepare the United States for the conflict. Sometime around the end of spring and beginning of summer, possibly after the Republican Party nominated Wendell Willkie as its presidential candidate, Roosevelt made up his mind to run again. Then he set out to get the nomination. He did it with an astounding political maneuver: He said he didn't want to run.

————————— ✧ —————————

Willkie, the Republican candidate, appealed to some Democrats who thought Roosevelt was abusing his power.

"WE WANT ROOSEVELT!"

On the night of July 16, 1940, Senator Alben Barkley of Kentucky stoked the crowd at the Chicago Democratic National Convention with a speech about the New Deal. The crowd erupted with joy when he mentioned Roosevelt's name. Then he stunned the crowd into silence by reading a message from the president: "You and my other close friends have known and understood that I have not today and have never had any wish or purpose to remain in the office of president."

In the middle of the stunned silence, one of Roosevelt's supporters—a city sewer employee hidden in the basement by Chicago's mayor Ed Kelly—began to chant, "We want Roosevelt!" by shouting into a sound system. The voice echoed through loudspeakers in the convention hall and the crowd caught fire. "We want Roosevelt! Everybody wants Roosevelt! The world needs Roosevelt!" Delegates paraded with their state flags. Spectators, arranged by Mayor Kelly, joined in. Chaos engulfed the hall.

In the meantime, Roosevelt's aides worked furiously. They needed to gather enough votes from delegates to ensure a landslide first ballot. They succeeded.

"When the conflict first broke out last September [1939], it was still my intention to announce . . . at an early date, that under no conditions would I accept reelection," Roosevelt declared in a radio address to the convention. The "conflict" was World War II. "It soon became evident, however, that such a public statement on my part would be unwise from the point of view of sheer public duty."

Republican Willkie spoke of improving New Deal programs but did not attack them. Nor did he challenge

Roosevelt's stance against Germany until late in the campaign. The war gave Roosevelt a major advantage. "I would rather have FDR with his known faults than Willkie with his unknown qualities," said Republican mayor Fiorello LaGuardia of New York, summing up the majority view. The incumbent beat his opponent by nearly five million votes, taking 449 electoral votes to Willkie's 82.

THE THREAT LOOMS

Franklin faced the looming war both as president and father. At the end of September 1940, he took time out from running the country to host a birthday party for his son Elliott. Sitting at the head of the long table in Hyde Park, he raised his glass to his son, who had recently joined the U.S. Army Air Force as a captain.

———————————— ◇ ————————————

Eventually, all four of Franklin's sons joined the armed forces. Elliott (center) served in the air force, James (not pictured) was in the marines, and Franklin Jr. (right) and John (not pictured) were in the navy. The man on the left is not identified.

"To Elliott," said the president. "He's the first of the family to think seriously enough, and soberly enough, about the threat to America to join his country's Armed Services. We're all very proud of him, and I'm the proudest."

Meanwhile, President Roosevelt strengthened the U.S. military. He also helped Britain in its war against Germany. He loaned desperately needed destroyers (warships) to the British in return for military bases and future payments in a program called Lend-Lease. He ordered the U.S. Navy to patrol the Atlantic against German submarines, called U-boats, which made it possible for Britain to concentrate its small forces closer to home. He seized German and Italian merchant ships and established bases in Greenland. When Hitler invaded the Soviet Union in June 1941, Roosevelt began seeking ways to help the Soviets, even though they had once been allied with Germany.

A national poll in 1941 showed most people favored aiding Great Britain. Roosevelt knew, however, that Americans did not favor sending troops. They were reluctant even to increase the army and navy. He worked to change their minds. "We must be the great arsenal of democracy," he told the nation in a fireside address on December 29, 1940. "For us this is an emergency as serious as war itself."

CHAPTER EIGHT

INFAMY AND TRIUMPH

"It will not only be a long war, it will be a hard war. That is the basis on which we now lay all our plans."

—Franklin D. Roosevelt's address to the nation, December 9, 1941

On Sunday afternoon, December 7, 1941, President Roosevelt lunched with Harry Hopkins on the second floor of the White House. Hopkins had worked for Roosevelt in New York, helping to organize the TERA relief program. He had come to the administration as Federal Emergency Relief Administrator. After Louis Howe died in 1936, the president relied on Hopkins more and more. When World War II began in Europe, Hopkins traveled to Great Britain and the Soviet Union as Roosevelt's personal envoy.

The president and his aide had many things to discuss. American sanctions designed to punish Japan for invading Southeast Asia hurt the Japanese—but that only made them determined to conquer the rest of Asia. Negotiations were being held, but Roosevelt and Hopkins both knew they would be futile. A few days earlier, American intelligence agents had intercepted messages from the Japanese that clearly indicated they were planning more attacks. There was some debate about where the next attack would occur—the British and Dutch possessions near Southeast Asia were likely targets, as were the Philippine Islands.

Americans in the Philippines, Hawaii, and the South Pacific were put on alert. At the same time, Roosevelt made a final try for peace. He had sent a message to Emperor Hirohito of Japan on December 6. "The people of the United States, believing in peace and in the right of nations to live and let live . . . have hoped for a termination of the present conflict between Japan and China," he said. "We have hoped that a peace of the Pacific could be consummated in such a way that nationalities of many diverse people could exist side by side without fear of invasion." He asked the emperor to make one more attempt at peace.

But Roosevelt didn't feel much like talking about war with Hopkins that Sunday. He hoped to get through their business quickly, then spend the rest of the afternoon working on his stamp collection. At about 2:00 P.M., the phone on Roosevelt's desk rang. The president picked it up. Secretary of the Navy Frank Knox was on the other line.

Radio reports from Honolulu, Hawaii, told of an air raid at nearby Pearl Harbor. "There must be some mistake," said Hopkins. The president's face turned ashen. He sensed immediately the far-fetched news was true. In an instant, he realized the outrageous boldness of the attack made it very possible. It would be just like the Japanese, he

Japanese bombs pour down on Pearl Harbor. Twenty-one ships sank or were destroyed, and more than 2,400 Americans died in the attack.

———————————— ◇ ————————————

told Hopkins, to attack at the "very time they were discussing peace."

The news got worse quickly. By 2:30, Roosevelt knew the U.S. Pacific Fleet had been devastated. A half-hour later, he called a meeting with the secretaries of war and the navy, along with others, to discuss the situation. Roosevelt shook his head with each report, amazed that his navy had been caught so totally by surprise.

"In spite of his anxiety, Franklin was in a way more

serene than he had appeared in a long time," Eleanor wrote later. "I think it was steadying to know finally that the die was cast. One could no longer do anything but face the fact that this country was in a war; from here on, difficult and dangerous as the future looked, it presented a clearer challenge than the long uncertainty of the past."

"HOSTILITIES EXIST"

The next day, Roosevelt walked slowly to the rostrum (platform) in the House chamber of the Capitol. In a firm, calm voice, he addressed Congress and the country. "Yesterday, December 7, 1941—a date which will live in infamy—the United States of America was suddenly and deliberately attacked by naval and air forces of the Empire of Japan. . . .

"Hostilities exist," said Roosevelt. "There is no blinking at the fact that our people, our territory, and our interests are in grave danger.

"With confidence in our armed forces—with the unbounding determination of our people—we will gain the inevitable triumph—so help us God."

──────────────── ✧

Roosevelt signs the U.S. declaration of war against Japan.

DID FDR KNOW?

Ever since the bombs stopped falling on Pearl Harbor (*above*) in December 1941, Americans have asked themselves how their navy could have been caught so unprepared. Soon after the attack, some began to blame Roosevelt. Since that time, various conspiracy theories have sprung up, accusing Roosevelt of knowing that the Japanese were planning the attack. According to some of these theories, Roosevelt deliberately withheld the information from his commanders.

Historians and Roosevelt biographers have shown this is nonsense. Among the points made by conspiracy theorists is the fact that the U.S. was intercepting Japanese secret codes. Roosevelt saw, or at least could have seen, the information in these messages. The theorists, however, rarely point out that the codes that were broken were diplomatic codes. These codes tipped Roosevelt off that Japan was getting ready for war. But they did not contain any information about where the attack would be. In fact, that information was deliberately kept secret from diplomats by the Japanese.

About a dozen messages relating to the attack were sent in a military code prior to the attack. Unfortunately, these messages were not decoded until after the war had ended. A navy investigation that took place afterward claimed that, had the messages been decoded at the time, the fleet could have been saved. However, there is reason to doubt even that claim. The Japanese were trying to divert attention from their plans in other ways. There is no guarantee the navy would have interpreted the messages properly even if they had been decoded. Most leaders felt Hawaii was too far away to be threatened. And history shows that even when a country knows an attack is coming, it is difficult to properly prepare.

Another variation of the conspiracy theories charges that Roosevelt and America "forced" Japan to attack by imposing economic sanctions. The sanctions were imposed only after repeated Japanese aggression and advances in Asia. Saying that the sanctions made Japan attack America is a little like a bully claiming a person who said "don't hit me" started a fight.

AMERICAN ASSISTANCE

Almost immediately, Germany and Italy joined Japan in declaring war on the United States. These countries formed the Axis powers. The countries united against them were called the Allies, or Allied Forces. The alliances in one of the greatest wars of all time were now set.

The Constitution made Roosevelt the commander in chief of the army and navy. He relied heavily on General George Marshall, the army chief of staff, and Admiral Ernest J. King, the commander in chief of the United States Fleet, to organize and run the war. Both men were able and independent leaders. King knew how to use aircraft in naval warfare. This proved to be an important skill, critical to American strategy in the Pacific. Marshall built the U.S. Army from a small, ill-equipped force into the greatest power the world had ever known.

UNITED WE STAND

Roosevelt believed that close cooperation between the United States and Great Britain would be one of the keys to winning the war. And one of the best ways to accomplish that was by maintaining a good relationship with Prime Minister Winston Churchill of Great Britain. The men had begun corresponding before the war began in Europe and were good friends by the time of Pearl Harbor. Churchill sailed to Washington at the end of December 1941. Among other things, the two leaders established a high-level group of generals from both countries to help them run the war. They reaffirmed their stance against the Axis powers and their willingness to join with the other Allied Forces to fight them.

Roosevelt and Winston Churchill (above) *began corresponding in 1939. Churchill felt it was important to cultivate the United States as an ally.*

Roosevelt traveled several times during the war to meet with Churchill and the Soviet Union's leader, Joseph Stalin. These face-to-face meetings took him by airplane and ship to Cairo, Egypt, and to Tehran, Iran. Roosevelt felt it was important for the world leaders to meet and discuss war issues face to face.

THE TURNING TIDE

As 1942 began, the outlook seemed bleak. Germany renewed its offensive in Russia. Japan continued its conquest of Asia. Fear of enemy spies and saboteurs and anti-Japanese hysteria in the United States led Roosevelt to sign an order in February 1942. The order removed West Coast people of Japanese ancestry from their homes and

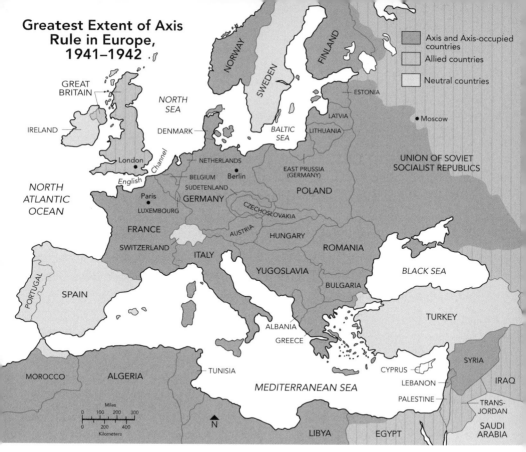

Axis and Axis-occupied countries

Allied countries

Neutral countries

GREAT BRITAIN

NORTH SEA

NORWAY

SWEDEN

FINLAND

ESTONIA

LATVIA

LITHUANIA

Moscow

IRELAND

DENMARK

BALTIC SEA

London

NETHERLANDS

EAST PRUSSIA (GERMANY)

UNION OF SOVIET SOCIALIST REPUBLICS

English Channel

BELGIUM

Berlin

POLAND

NORTH ATLANTIC OCEAN

Paris

SUDETENLAND

GERMANY

LUXEMBOURG

CZECHOSLOVAKIA

FRANCE

AUSTRIA

HUNGARY

SWITZERLAND

ITALY

ROMANIA

YUGOSLAVIA

BLACK SEA

PORTUGAL

SPAIN

BULGARIA

TURKEY

ALBANIA

GREECE

CYPRUS

SYRIA

MOROCCO

ALGERIA

TUNISIA

MEDITERRANEAN SEA

LEBANON

PALESTINE

IRAQ

TRANS-JORDAN

Miles

Kilometers

N

LIBYA

EGYPT

SAUDI ARABIA

This map shows Axis occupation in Europe and northern Africa at its height in 1941 and 1942.

placed them in inland internment camps. His order stripped them of most of their rights and much of their property, even though two-thirds of the 117,000 internees were American citizens. Many stayed behind barbed wire for most of the war.

At the time, American anger toward anything Japanese, even fellow citizens, was immense. Rumors of impending attacks against the West Coast filled newspapers and radio stations. Still, the injustice of arresting American citizens and taking their property without trial or just cause would go down as a dark mark in history.

As 1942 continued, momentum in the war began to turn in favor of the Allies. The U.S. Navy defeated a major Japanese carrier force near Midway Island in the Pacific in June, sinking four aircraft carriers and a heavy cruiser. The battle, the first in history to be fought almost entirely by airplanes, stopped the Japanese advance in the Pacific. Gradually, the situation improved for the Allies. The Soviets stopped the German attacks. British and American forces launched an offensive in North Africa in 1942, then went on to Italy.

INDUSTRY GEARS UP

World War II stoked the American economy. Factories churned out weapons of all kinds. The lean years gave way to a boom. Many New Deal programs expired because they were no longer needed. Still, Roosevelt wanted to extend prosperity to everyone in society and to guarantee that good economic times would continue after the war. Among the measures he backed to do that was the GI Bill of Rights. Signed into law in June 1944, the bill provided veterans with college tuition and mortgage guarantees. These programs enabled millions of veterans to attend college and buy homes, changing middle-class America after the war.

Besides running the federal government, Roosevelt kept up on local affairs in Hyde Park. Still a vestryman, he consulted with other church members about a new rector in 1943. He even joked that he might preside over a service himself when home. "I have done it on board ship in my capacity of Senior Officer present," he told W. Russell Bowie in a letter dated February 6, 1943, "but I was not much of a success."

D-DAY

"The first of the Axis capitals is now in our hand!" Roosevelt told Americans in his June 5, 1944, fireside chat, announcing that Rome, Italy, had been liberated. "One up and two to go!"

Roosevelt's happy voice betrayed none of the anxiety he felt. At that moment, thousands of Allied troops were crossing the English Channel to land on the beaches of Normandy in France. The D-Day operation was the largest and among the riskiest of the war. Defeat on the beaches would be disastrous, but it was a risk that had to be taken.

Roosevelt went to bed immediately after his broadcast. At 3:00 A.M., Eleanor woke him. He pulled on a sweater and

———————————— ✧ ————————————

A boat full of U.S. troops approaches a beach in Normandy on D-Day.

reached anxiously for the phone next to his bed. The troops, General Marshall told him, were ashore and advancing.

Roosevelt had every member of the staff report to duty at once. The entire nation seemed to realize the importance of the invasion and the difficulty of the moment. As historian Stephen Ambrose puts it, "The impulse to pray was overwhelming."

Roosevelt met with members of Congress, his advisers, and military leaders as the day went on. It soon became clear that the Americans had won a great victory, though of course much remained to be done. "You just don't land on a beach and walk through . . . to Berlin," the president told reporters. "And the quicker this country understands it the better."

Roosevelt was certainly right. One million troops and 171,532 vehicles would go ashore in France in the next three weeks. But the German army was far from defeated, and Japan remained in control of much of the Pacific.

TRUMAN

Many times that spring and summer, Roosevelt hoped the war would end quickly. One of his reasons was personal—he didn't want to run for reelection. His health had begun to decline. He had lost weight, and his energy often sagged. But Roosevelt and many others believed stepping down in the middle of the war would be too disruptive, so he decided to seek a fourth term—but with a new vice president.

Vice President Henry Wallace was under severe attack for being too liberal. More important, Roosevelt doubted Wallace's ability to lead the country. So he settled on Senator Harry S. Truman of Missouri as his running mate,

Harry S. Truman
——————— ◇ ———————

even though Truman was not a staunch Roosevelt supporter.

After the Democratic convention, Roosevelt traveled to Hawaii to meet with his army and navy commanders to plan the final American drive against Japan. While there, the president took time out to visit a hospital full of wounded servicemen. He told his Secret Service men to wheel him through the amputee ward slowly and to pass each bed. It was one of the few times the president showed himself to strangers while in his wheelchair.

"He wanted to display himself and his useless legs to those boys who would have to face the same bitterness," said aide Sam Rosenman. Roosevelt smiled for the men, but as he was wheeled out, tears filled his eyes.

THE OLD MASTER

As fall 1944 began, Roosevelt turned his attention to politics. Republican challenger Thomas Dewey had been running a strong campaign. Roosevelt suffered from heart trouble, and for the first time there seemed a real possibility he might lose a presidential election. "Has the old master still got it?" asked *Time* magazine. In October two newspapers questioned his health in front-page editorials.

Once more, Roosevelt fought back. Even though the weather was terrible, he launched an open-car campaign to demonstrate that he wasn't sick. As many as three million New Yorkers gathered in the rain to throw ticker tape on him and Eleanor as they paraded up Broadway in his car. The campaign reached its climax in Chicago before 110,000 screaming supporters inside Soldier Field and another 150,000 outside. Roosevelt joked that the Republicans were saying that the country needed a change from its "quarrelsome tired old men" but then admitted they wouldn't change anything the tired old men were doing. Roosevelt went on to remind his listeners of what he called his economic bill of rights, which included the right to a job, education, and health care. These were the same rights granted veterans in the GI Bill.

"Some people," he told the crowd, " . . . have sneered at these ideals. . . . They have said that they were the dreams of starry-eyed New Dealers, that it is silly to talk of them because we cannot attain these ideals tomorrow or the next day. The American people have greater faith than that. I know that they agree with these objectives—that they demand them—that they are determined to get them—and that they are going to get them. The American people have a good habit—the habit of going right ahead and accomplishing the impossible."

Roosevelt's victory was his narrowest, but it was still a landslide. He received 53.5 percent of the popular vote to Dewey's 46 percent and dominated the electoral college, 432 to 99.

"A LITTLE SLEEP"

On January 20, 1945, Franklin Roosevelt stood on the south portico (porch) of the White House. In the bitter cold, he took his oath of office for the fourth time. There were no crowds and no parades. The ceremony seemed almost private. The official reason was the war, but Roosevelt's rapidly declining health was also a factor.

"There was a drawn, almost ethereal [otherworldly] look about him," remembered his son James. "At times the old zestfulness was there, but often—particularly when he let down his guard—he seemed thousands of miles away."

Roosevelt put on his cheerful smile for the others at the reception after the ceremony. His health had declined sharply after the presidential campaign and maybe partly

———————————— ✧ ————————————

Roosevelt gives his inaugural address at the White House.
His speech was only five minutes long.

The Big Three—Roosevelt (center), *Churchill* (left), *and Stalin*
(right)—*meet at Yalta to discuss plans for the last phases of the war.*

because of it. In February he sailed to Yalta, a Soviet resort
city on the Black Sea, for another meeting with Churchill
and Stalin. His interpreter said he was "in top form as a
charming host, witty conversationalist, with the spark and
light in his eyes and that gracious smile which always won
people over to him." In private moments, though, the president faded.

On the way home, he discussed the atomic bomb with
Churchill. As early as 1939, Roosevelt had approved federal programs to develop it. He had also reserved to himself
the authority to drop it. The president told the prime minister it would be ready for testing around September.

Germany stood on the brink of collapse, though surrender was still months away. The war with Japan was going
well, but its end was not yet in sight. "Headed in the right
direction," Roosevelt wrote his wife as he sailed home aboard
the U.S.S. *Quincy*. "All well, but still need a little sleep."

On March 30, Roosevelt arrived in Warm Springs for a
working vacation. Driving through the countryside in his

car, he felt the warm sun invigorate him. But his failing health was obvious. His hands trembled as he poured cocktails. He couldn't lift himself from his wheelchair to a seat.

On the afternoon of April 12, 1945, Roosevelt sat in his favorite leather chair by the fireplace. Letters and papers were spread out nearby. At 1:30 P.M., the sixty-two-year-old president said, "I have a headache" and slumped over. He had suffered a massive cerebral hemorrhage.

A few hours later, Eleanor sent a telegram to her sons serving in the armed forces. It said, "Darlings: Pa slipped away this afternoon. He did his job to the end as he would want you to do. Bless you. All our love."

——————————————— ✧ ———————————————

The president's coffin passes through the streets of Washington, D.C. Roosevelt was later buried at Hyde Park.

WORLD WAR II

While the United States did not enter World War II until after Japan bombed Pearl Harbor, the other major world powers had been fighting since the late 1930s. Europe and much of Asia, northern Africa, and parts of the Middle East were devastated in the conflict.

Germany, Italy, and Japan formed the Axis powers. Fighting against them were the Allies, which included Great Britain and France, and eventually the United States. The Germans invaded and conquered France in 1940. The Soviet Union, allied with Germany during the invasion of Poland in 1939, was attacked by the Germans in 1941 and then joined the Allies.

Germany surrendered on May 7, 1945, less than a month after Roosevelt died. Harry S. Truman succeeded Roosevelt as president and oversaw the end of the war. Truman met with Churchill and Stalin in Potsdam, Germany, in July to tell them about the successful test of the atomic bomb that had occurred earlier that month. On August 6, an American B-29 bomber dropped the first atomic bomb used in warfare on the Japanese city of Hiroshima. Three days later, the United States dropped a second bomb on Nagasaki, Japan. On August 14, the Japanese agreed to end the war. They signed the official statement of surrender on September 2. The Axis countries were occupied by the victors for several years, and the effects of World War II are still felt.

The casualties (dead, wounded, or missing in action) from the war were literally uncountable but totaled far into the millions. During World War II, German leader Adolf Hitler launched the Holocaust, murdering at least six million Jews in concentration camps. The war began with some troops fighting on horseback. It ended with the use of the atomic bomb, opening the gates to the nuclear age.

TIMELINE

1882 Franklin Delano Roosevelt is born at Springside, Hyde Park, in New York on January 30.

1896 Franklin enters Groton School, near Boston, Massachusetts.

1900 Franklin enters Harvard University. Franklin's father, James Roosevelt, dies.

1903 Franklin becomes engaged to Eleanor Roosevelt.

1904 Franklin enters Columbia Law School.

1905 Franklin and Eleanor marry on March 17.

1906 Anna Eleanor Roosevelt is born on May 3.

1907 Franklin passes his law exams and works for the firm of Carter, Ledyard, and Milburn. James Roosevelt is born on December 23.

1909 Franklin Jr. is born on March 18 but dies later that year.

1910 Franklin is elected to the New York state senate. Elliott Roosevelt is born on September 23.

1912 Franklin is reelected to the senate.

1913 President Woodrow Wilson appoints Franklin assistant secretary of the navy.

1914 Franklin loses the New York Democratic primary for the U.S. Senate. A second Franklin Jr. is born on August 17.

1916 John Aspinwall Roosevelt is born on March 13.

1917 The United States enters World War I.

1920 The Democratic Party names Franklin its vice presidential candidate.

1921 Franklin contracts polio. He will never walk again.

1924 Franklin nominates Al Smith for president at the Democratic National Convention.

1926 Franklin purchases Warm Springs, a resort in Georgia.

1928 Franklin is elected governor of New York.

1929 The United States enters the Great Depression. Franklin works to bring relief to the unemployed.

1930 Franklin wins reelection as governor.

1932 Franklin is elected president of the United States.

1933 Franklin begins stabilizing the country's financial system and begins the New Deal programs.

1935 The Social Security Act, one of Franklin's most important legacies, passes Congress.

1936 Roosevelt wins reelection to the presidency.

1940 Roosevelt is reelected to a third term.

1941 Sara Delano Roosevelt dies. Japan attacks Pearl Harbor. America enters World War II.

1943 Franklin meets with Churchill and Stalin in Tehran, Iran.

1944 Allied forces land in Normandy. Franklin wins reelection for a fourth term.

1945 Franklin meets with Churchill and Stalin at Yalta. Franklin dies of a cerebral hemorrhage in Warm Springs, Georgia, on April 12.

Source Notes

10 Kenneth S. Davis, *FDR: The Beckoning of Destiny, 1882–1928* (New York: G. P. Putnam's Sons, 1972), 36.

12 Geoffrey C. Ward, *Before the Trumpet* (New York: Harper & Row, 1985), 113

12 Ibid., 154.

13 Ibid., 156.

14–15 Ibid., 164.

20 Eleanor Roosevelt, *This Is My Story* (New York: Harper & Brothers, 1937), 5.

20 Ted Morgan, *FDR: A Biography* (New York: Simon & Schuster, 1985), 94.

20 Eleanor Roosevelt, *This Is My Story,* 24.

20 Ibid., 111.

22 Davis, *The Beckoning of Destiny,* 153.

24 Ibid., 199.

25 Eleanor Roosevelt, *This Is My Story,* 165.

26 Davis, *The Beckoning of Destiny,* 267.

28 Ibid., 305.

29 Ibid., 489.

30 Ibid., 623.

32–33 Hugh Gregory Gallagher, *FDR's Splendid Deception* (New York: Dodd, Mead & Company, 1985), 4.

36 Ibid., 222.

36 Eleanor Roosevelt, *This Is My Story,* 328.

36 Kenneth S. Davis, *FDR: The War President, 1940–1943* (New York: Random House, 2000), 39.

36 Gallagher, p. 64.

37 Elliott Roosevelt and James Brough, *An Untold Story: The Roosevelts of Hyde Park* (New York: G. P. Putnam's Sons, 1973), 184.

37 Ibid.

37 Davis, *The War President,* 5.

37 Ibid., 6.

38 Geoffrey C. Ward, *A First Class Temperament* (New York: Harper & Row, 1989), 785.

44–45 Frank Freidel, *Franklin D. Roosevelt: A Rendezvous with Destiny* (Boston: Little, Brown and Company, 1990), 52.

45 Ibid.

45 Ward, *A First Class Temperament,* 792.

45 Kenneth S. Davis, *FDR: The New York Years, 1928–1933* (New York: Random House, 1985), 29.

46 Ibid., 30.

46 Ibid.

46 Ibid.

46 William A. DeGregorio, *The Complete Book of U.S. Presidents* (New York: Wings Books, 1991), 468.

48 Ward, *A First Class Temperament,* 796.

49 Roosevelt and Brough, *An Untold Story,* 177.

49 Eleanor Roosevelt, *This I Remember* (New York: Harper & Brothers, 1949), 56.

49–50 Elliott Roosevelt, ed., *F.D.R., His Personal Letters, 1928–1945,* 2 vols. (New York: Duell, Sloan and Pearce, 1950), 1:135.

54 Alfred B. Rollins Jr., *Roosevelt and Howe* (New York: Alfred A. Knopf, 1962), 293.

54 Freidel, 65.

54–55 Ibid., 70.

56 Ted Morgan, *FDR: A Biography* (New York: Simon & Schuster, 1985), 361.

57 Davis, *The New York Years,* 319.

58 Eleanor Roosevelt, *This I Remember,* 69.

59 Roosevelt and Brough, *An Untold Story,* 285–295.

59 Ibid., 293.

59 John Gabriel Hunt, *The Essential Franklin Delano Roosevelt* (New York: Gramercy Books, 1995), 29.

59–60 Roosevelt and Brough, *An Untold Story,* 295.

60 Ibid., 293.
61 First Inaugural Address of Franklin D. Roosevelt, gathered by The Avalon Project at the Yale Law School <http://www.yale.edu /lawweb/avalon/presiden/inaug /froos1.htm> (June 15, 2001).
61–62 Ibid.
62 Ibid.
63 Ibid.
63 Stanley Lebergott, *The Americans: An Economic Record* (New York: W. W. Norton, 1984), 447.
63 Russell D. Buhite and David W. Levy, eds. *FDR's Fireside Chats* (Norman, OK: University of Oklahoma Press, 1992), 12.,
64–65 Freidel, 99.
66 Peter Collier, *The Roosevelts: An American Saga* (New York: Simon & Schuster, 1994), 371.
67 Eleanor Roosevelt, *This I Remember,* 81.
69 Ibid., 117.
69 Collier, 352.
69 Ibid., 353.
70 Kenneth S. Davis, *FDR: The New Deal Years, 1933–1937* (New York: Random House, 1986), 437.
72 Hunt, 93.
73 Arthur M. Schlesinger Jr., *The Coming of the New Deal* (Boston: Houghton Mifflin Company, 1959), 311.
73 Davis, *The New Deal Years*, 523.
74 Arthur M. Schlesigner, *The Politics of Upheaval* (Boston: Houghton Mifflin, 1960), 634.
75 Ibid., 638.
75 Ibid., 639.
76 Ibid.
76 Buhite and Levy, 86.
76–77 Ibid., 89.
77 Freidel, 232.
77 John Costello, *The Pacific War* (New York: Quill, 1981), 47.
77 Elliott Roosevelt, ed., *His Personal Letters,* 1:530.
79 Ibid., 2:801.

79 Ibid., 802.
79 Morgan, 519.
80 Eleanor Roosevelt, *This I Remember,* 212.
80 Morgan, 529.
81 Kenneth S. Davis, *FDR: Into the Storm, 1937–1940* (New York: Random House, 1993), 597.
81 Hunt, 181–182.
81 Morgan, 540.
82 Collier, 377.
82–83 Buhite and Levy, 173.
83 Hunt, 232.
85 Robert E. Sherwood, *Roosevelt and Hopkins* (New York: Harper & Brothers, 1948), 431.
85 Ibid.
86 Eleanor Roosevelt, *This I Remember,* 233.
86–87 Hunt, 235–237.
87 Elliott Roosevelt, *His Personal Letters,* 2:1399.
93 Buhite and Levy, 295.
94 Stephen Ambrose, *D-Day* (New York: Simon & Schuster, 1994), 495.
95 Doris Kearns Goodwin, *No Ordinary Time* (New York: Simon & Schuster, 1994), 510.
95 Ibid., 532.
96 Freidel, 557.
97 James MacGregor Burns, *Roosevelt: The Soldier of Freedom* (New York: Konecky & Konecky, 1970), 527.
97 Jim Bishop, *F.D.R.'s Last Year* (New York: William Morrow & Company, 1974), 182.
97 James Roosevelt and Sidney Shalett, *Affectionately, F.D.R.* (New York: Harcourt, Brace & Company, 1959), 354.
98 Roosevelt and Shalett, 357.
99 Elliott Roosevelt, *His Personal Letters,* 2:1571.
100 Freidel, 605.
100 Roosevelt and Shalett, 361.
100 Ibid.

BIBLIOGRAPHY

Ambrose, Stephen. *D-Day*. New York: Simon & Schuster, 1994.

Asbell, Bernard. *The F.D.R. Memoirs*. Garden City, NY: Doubleday & Company, 1973.

Bishop, Jim. *FDR's Last Year*. New York: William Morrow & Company, 1974.

Buhite, Russell D., and David W. Levy, eds. *FDR's Fireside Chats*. Norman, OK: University of Oklahoma Press, 1992.

Burns, James MacGregor. *Roosevelt: The Soldier of Freedom*. New York: Konecky & Konecky, 1970.

Collier, Peter. *The Roosevelts: An American Saga*. New York: Simon & Schuster, 1994.

Costello, John. *The Pacific War 1941–1945*. New York: Quill, 1982.

Davis, Kenneth S. *FDR: The Beckoning of Destiny, 1882–1928*. New York: G. P. Putnam's Sons, 1972.

———. *FDR: Into the Storm, 1937–1940*. New York: Random House, 1993.

———. *FDR: The New Deal Years, 1933–1937*. New York: Random House, 1986.

———. *FDR: The New York Years, 1928–1933*. New York: Random House, 1985.

———. *FDR: The War President, 1940–1943*. New York: Random House, 2000.

DeGregorio, William A. *The Complete Book of U.S. Presidents*. New York: Wings Books, 1991.

Fehrenbach, T. R. *F.D.R.'s Undeclared War, 1939–1941*. New York: David McKay Company, 1967.

Freidel, Frank. *Franklin D. Roosevelt: A Rendezvous with Destiny*. Boston: Little, Brown and Company, 1990.

Galbraith, John Kenneth. *The Great Crash*. Boston: Houghton Mifflin, 1988.

Gallagher, Hugh Gregory. *FDR's Splendid Deception.* New York: Dodd, Mead & Company, 1985.

Gilbert, Martin. *The Second World War.* New York: Henry Holt and Company, 1989.

Goodwin, Doris Kearns. *No Ordinary Time.* New York: Simon & Schuster, 1994.

Hickok, Lorena. *One Third of a Nation.* Edited by Richard Lowitt and Maurine Beasley. Urbana, IL: University of Illinois Press, 1981.

Hoyt, Edwin P. *Japan's War.* New York: McGraw-Hill Book Company, 1986.

Hunt, John Gabriel, ed. *The Essential Franklin Delano Roosevelt.* New York: Gramercy Books, 1995.

Lash, Joseph P. *Roosevelt and Churchill, 1939–1941.* New York: W. W. Norton & Company, 1976.

————. *A World of Love.* Garden City, NY: Doubleday & Company, 1984.

Lebergott, Stanley. *The Americans: An Economic Record.* New York: W. W. Norton, 1984.

Morgan, Ted. *FDR: A Biography.* New York: Simon & Schuster, 1985.

Prange, Gordon W. *At Dawn We Slept.* New York: McGraw Hill, 1981.

Rollins, Alfred B. Jr. *Roosevelt and Howe.* New York: Alfred A. Knopf, 1962.

Roosevelt, Eleanor. *This I Remember.* New York: Harper & Brothers, 1949.

————. *This Is My Story.* New York: Harper & Brothers, 1937.

Roosevelt, Elliott, ed. *F.D.R., His Personal Letters, 1928–1945.* 2 vols. New York: Duell, Sloan and Pearce, 1950.

Roosevelt, Elliott, and James Brough. *An Untold Story: The Roosevelts of Hyde Park.* New York: G. P. Putnam's Sons, 1973.

Roosevelt, Franklin D. *The Public Papers of Franklin D. Roosevelt.* Vol. IV, 1935. New York: Russell & Russell, 1938.

Roosevelt, James, and Sidney Shalett. *Affectionately, F.D.R.* New York: Harcourt, Brace & Company, 1959.

Schlesinger, Arthur M. Jr. *The Coming of the New Deal.* Boston: Houghton Mifflin, 1959.

———. *The Crisis of the Old Order.* Boston: Houghton Mifflin, 1957.

———. *The Politics of Upheaval.* Boston: Houghton Mifflin, 1960.

Sherwood, Robert E. *Roosevelt and Hopkins.* New York: Harper & Brothers, 1948.

Terkel, Studs. *Hard Times.* New York: Pantheon Books, 1970.

Ward, Geoffrey C. *Before the Trumpet.* New York: Harper & Row, 1985.

———. *A First Class Temperament.* New York: Harper & Row, 1989.

Weinberg, Gerhard L. *A World at Arms.* Cambridge, England: Cambridge University Press, 1994.

FURTHER READING AND WEBSITES

Damon, Duane. *Headin' for Better Times: The Arts of the Great Depression.* Minneapolis: Lerner Publications Company, 2002.

Devaney, John. *Franklin Delano Roosevelt, President.* New York: Walker and Co., 1987.

Fireside Chats of Franklin D. Roosevelt. <http://www.mhric.org/fdr/fdr.html>. The texts of Franklin D. Roosevelt's fireside chats are available at this website.

Franklin D. Roosevelt Presidential Library and Museum. <http://www.fdrlibrary.marist.edu/>. This website features biographies of Franklin and Eleanor Roosevelt, as well as information about the library and museum in Hyde Park, New York.

Freedman, Russell. *Franklin Delano Roosevelt.* New York: Clarion Books, 1990.

Fremon, David K. *The Great Depression in American History.* Springfield, NJ: Enslow Publishers, 1997.

Josephson, Judith Pinkerton. *Growing Up in World War II, 1941 to 1945.* Minneapolis: Lerner Publications Company, 2003.

Larsen, Rebecca. *Franklin Roosevelt: Man of Destiny.* New York: Franklin Watts, 1991.

Lazo, Caroline Evenson. *Harry S. Truman.* Minneapolis: Lerner Publications Company, 2003.

New Deal Network. <http://newdeal.feri.org/>. This website offers additional information about Franklin D. Roosevelt, the Great Depression, and the New Deal.

Selfridge, John W. *Franklin D. Roosevelt, The People's President.* New York: Fawcett Columbine, 1990.

Whitman, Sylvia. *V Is for Victory: The American Home Front during World War II.* Minneapolis: Lerner Publications Company, 1993.

Winget, Mary. *Eleanor Roosevelt.* Minneapolis: Lerner Publications Company, 2001.

INDEX

ABOUT THE AUTHOR

Before writing books for young readers, Jeremy Roberts worked as a political reporter in New York. He spent several years in the Hudson Valley and came to know many people who had once known and worked with Franklin D. Roosevelt.

This book is dedicated to his grandparents and all the other people Franklin D. Roosevelt helped during the Great Depression.

PHOTO ACKNOWLEDGMENTS

The images in this book are used with the permission of:
The White House, pp. 1, 7, 9, 17, 35, 43, 53, 61, 71, 84; Franklin D. Roosevelt Library, pp. 2, 6, 11 (both), 13, 14, 15, 19, 21, 23, 24, 31, 32, 34, 38, 39, 40, 41, 44, 47, 52, 55, 56, 62, 64, 66, 68, 73, 75, 80, 82, 86, 98; Dictionary of American Portraits, p. 18; Army War College, courtesy of Franklin D. Roosevelt Library, p. 29; Franklin D. Roosevelt Library, photo by Margaret Suckley, p. 37; Library of Congress, pp. 48 (LC-USZ62-33277), 100 (LC-USZ62-67439); AP/ Wide World Photos, pp. 60, 96; Fitzpatrick in the *St. Louis Post-Dispatch*, photo courtesy of State Historical Society of Missouri, Columbia, p. 78; National Archives, pp. 87 (79-AR-82), 88 (80-G-32420), 99 (111-SC-260486); Southdale-Hennepin Area Library, p. 91; Laura Westlund, p. 92; Illustrated London News, p. 94.

Front cover: courtesy of the Franklin D. Roosevelt Library.